SEO LAW

How can the Australian Consumer Law and Intellectual Property Law be used to regulate the Black Hat SEO used by SEO companies, in order to better protect online consumers and small business owners?

First Edition

SEO LAW

How can the Australian Consumer Law and Intellectual Property Law be used to regulate the Black Hat SEO used by SEO companies, in order to better protect online consumers and small business owners?

by

ADRIENNE PARK

Supervisor & Proofreader: Aidan Booker

Course Convenor: Associate Professor Therese Wilson

November 2016 : First Edition

Contact : info@jinslegalstory.com

See: *http://www.jinslegalstory.com/seo-law/* for release details.

The Law Research Elective (LRE) is an elective course that provides an opportunity for students to undertake a major piece of self-directed research in an area of their choice. Working closely with a supervisor in the Griffith Law School, the student produces a 5000 word research paper in one semester. The student assumes no responsibility for errors or omission or for damages resulting from the use of the information in this book.

ISBN: 978-0-9953801-1-0

TABLE OF CONTENTS

ABSTRACT

GOOGLE CREATED THE NEED FOR Search Engine Optimisation ('SEO') and SEO professionals to help increase website ranking among more than one million websites in Google. There are three types of SEO strategies: White Hat SEO ('WHSEO'), Black Hat SEO ('BHSEO'), and Grey Hat SEO('GHSEO'). While there is no clear legal definition of WHSEO, it can be explained as a positive SEO strategy, operated by a human, which improves the search engine performance on a SERP.[1] BHSEO strategies are the opposite of WHSEO and include cybersquatting, abusing meta tags, creating fake reviews to receive backlinks, sending fake website traffic, content farms and using spammy linkbuilding methods.[2] The reasons a business owner may pursue BHSEO are for the advantages of cost efficiency, requiring short periods of time to increase PR, and the campaigns are easy to maintain by software.[3] Unfortunately, there are many SEO companies that fail to reach their intended achievement within a certain period of time. This may result in engaging in misleading or deceptive conduct under the *Australian Consumer Law ('ACL')* or a breach of *Intercultural Property Law ('IPL')*.

1 Evan Bailyn and Bardley Bailyn, *Outsmarting Google: SEO Secrets to Winning New Business* (Que Publishing, 2011) 151-154.

2 Evan Bailyn and Bradley Bailyn, *Outsmarting Google: SEO Secrets to Winning New Business* (Que Publishing, 2011) 146-151.

3 Sean Odom, *Seo for 2011: Search Engine Optimization Secrets* (MediaWorksPublising.com, 2010) 210 -211.

1. INTRODUCTION

IN 1991, THERE WAS ONLY one website. It was known as the World Wide Web and was invented by Tim Berners-Lee.[4] According to the results of a survey by Netcraft, there are now, in 21st century over one billion websites on the World Wide Web.[5] Since Google was launched in 1998, it has become the world number one search engine site. Although, Google created the need for Search Engine Optimisation ('SEO') and SEO professionals to help increase website ranking among more than one million websites in Google, the term 'Search Engine Optimisation' appeared before Google was established. It is possible that the term was first used by John Audette in a meeting with Danny Sullivan in 1997 or in the same year by Bruce Clay, these people being the first practitioners of the SEO internet skill.[6] Throughout the history of SEO use, many issues have been raised due to the use of Black Hat SEO ('BHSEO') which delivers poor website rankings for small business owners and their clients. This research paper will discuss what White Hat SEO ('WHSEO') and BHSEO are. In particular, it will review and analyse if there are problems with BHSEO strategies under

---

4 Moschovitis Group Staff, *Internet: A Historical Encyclopedia* (ABC-CLIO, 2005) 15.

5 Netcraft, September 2016 Web Server Survey (9 September 2016) <https://news.netcraft.com/archives/category/web-server-survey/>. According to the results of a survey by Netcraft in 2016, there are 1,285,759,146 sites on the World Wide Web.

6 Zlatko Bezhovski, 'The Historical Development of Search Engine Optimization', (2015) 5(12) *Information and Knowledge Management* 92.

the current *Australian Consumer Law* ('*ACL*')[7] and Australian *Intellectual Property Law* ('*IPL*'). The paper will also suggest possible reforms in order to further protect business owners and online consumers in the current online market.

7 Schedule 2 of the *Competition and Consumer Act 2010* (Cth) (previously the *Trade Practices Act 1974*).

2. DEFINITION OF SEARCH ENGINE OPTIMISATION

SEO IS AN ABBREVIATION FOR "Search Engine Optimisation", which involves strategies that naturally increases website traffic and place a website in the Search Engine Results Page ('SERP') in response to the search queries of users.[8] This section will discuss what SEO is, types of BHSEO and some significant issues of using BHSEO in the Australian market. There are three types of SEO strategies: WHSEO, BHSEO, and Grey Hat SEO ('GHSEO'). While there is no clear legal definition of WHSEO, it can be explained as a positive SEO strategy, operated by a human, which improves the search engine performance on a SERP.[9] Some examples of WHSEO strategies are press releases, social media campaigns, article submissions to high Page Rank ('PR')[10] websites and Google AdWords campaigns.

---

8 Todd Perkins, *Search Engine Optimization for Flash: Best practices for using Flash on the web* ("O'Reilly Media, Inc.", 2009) 2. Search Engine Results Page, also known as SERP, is a page that displays search results on search engines sites such as Google, Yahoo and Bing.

9 Evan Bailyn and Bardley Bailyn, *Outsmarting Google: SEO Secrets to Winning New Business* (Que Publishing, 2011) 151–154.

10 The founders of Google, Larry Page and Sergey Brin developed the PageRank. PageRank has the different levels to measure the popularity of websites, ranging 0 to 10, depending on the page's importance and reliability. Google trusts and displays websites which have high levels of PageRank. This metric directly affects a website's search engine ranking.

Similar to WHSEO, there is no clear legal definition of BHSEO. Another name for BHSEO is "Unethical SEO".[11] BHSEO strategies are the opposite of WHSEO and include cybersquatting, abusing meta tags, creating fake reviews to receive backlinks, sending fake website traffic, content farms and using spammy linkbuilding methods.[12] The reason a business owner may pursue using BHSEO is for the advantages of cost efficiency, requiring short periods of time to increase PR, and the campaigns being easy to maintain by software.[13] In practice, WHSEO costs much more than BHSEO as it is manually operated by a human being compared with mostly being performed by software. Some SEO companies use BHSEO tactics to get quick results and payments from their clients.

Unfortunately, there are many SEO companies that fail to reach their intended achievement within a certain period of time. This can happen for many reasons.[14] Some SEO professionals do not have sufficient legal knowledge and may become involved in BHSEO through the use of certain software. This may result in engaging in misleading or deceptive conduct under the *ACL* or a breach of Intercultural Property Law.

---

11 F.Mbikiwa and M. Wdideman,' Implications of search engine spam on the visibility of South African e-commerce Web site' (2006) Vol 8(4) *South African Journal of Information Management.*

12 Evan Bailyn and Bradley Bailyn, *Outsmarting Google: SEO Secrets to Winning New Business* (Que Publishing, 2011) 146–151.

13 Sean Odom, *Seo for 2011: Search Engine Optimization Secrets* (MediaWorksPublising.com, 2010) 210 –211.

14 Brian Ainsley Horn, *Why Selling SEO is Unethical in 2016* (8 January 2016) <http://www.huffingtonpost.com/brian-horn/why-selling-seo-is-unethi_b_8929662.html>.

3. MISLEADING OR DECEPTIVE CONDUCTS UNDER THE AUSTRALIAN CONSUMER LAW

THIS SECTION WILL DISCUSS WHETHER conduct such as redirecting domain, cybersquatting abusing meta tags, creating fake reviews and sending fake website traffic, is misleading or deceptive conduct under the *ACL*. It will also discuss BHSEO strategies and analyse whether conduct where business owners use BHSEO tactics are misleading or deceptive conducts.

3.1 Redirecting Domain Name and Cybersquatting

One of the most common BHSEO strategies is to purchase a bulk batch of domain names and redirect customers to the original website using a 301 redirect[15] or 302 redirect function.[16] The Uniform Resource Locator ('URL') address is often changed or permanently moved from one page to another page while a website is migrated or updated. Redirects are then required to reach to a new page or new URL

15 Jon Rognerud, *Ultimate Guide to Search Engine Optimization: Drive Traffic, Boost Conversion Rates and Make Lots of Money* (Jon Rognerud SEO, 2008) 59-60; Mike Moran and Bill Hunt, *Search Engine Marketing, Inc.: Driving Search Traffic to Your Company's Website* (IBM Press, 2014) 289-290. A 301 redirect permanently redirects old URLs to a new URLs. A 301 redirect is the most common type of redirect that indicates to spiders and bots that they should visit a new page and crawl through the information on the page.

16 Ibid. Along with a 301 redirect, a 302 redirect is used for the temporary redirection.

address. Technically, it is called a "Sever-side Redirect".[17] A 404 error[18] often occurs as a result of broken links, which can seriously harm a website's ranking.[19] A 404 error will not only have a negative impact on web users, but also on web spiders since 404 error pages degrade the performance of a web spider.[20] To solve this issue, a 301 redirect is used. BHSEO experts intentionally purchase domain names with typographical errors. These become relevant when a web user accidentally inputs an incorrect website address into the search box on a search engine site. When this occurs, the user is hijacked and forced to visit the targeting website.[21] This is known as "typosquatting" or URL hijacking[22] which is a form of cybersquatting.

In the USA, "cybersquatting" is regulated under the *Anticybersquatting Consumer Protection Act* ('ACPA') which was enacted in 1999. This Act specifically targets cybersquatters who purchase and register domain names although they do not have any intention of using them.[23] Unlike the USA,

17 Jonathan Weber, *Practical Google Analytics and Google Tag Manager for Developers* (Apress, 2015) 186-187.

18 Scott Mitchell, *Designing Active Server Pages* ("O'Reilly Media, Inc.", 2000) 73-76. A 404 error page is showed when the page is not found on the server. The broken link pages should be fixed as quickly as possible as it impacts the website's ranking.

19 John Jerkovic, *SEO Warrior* ("O'Reilly Media, Inc.", 2009) 91-92.

20 B. Barla Cambazoglu and Ricardo Baeza-Yates, *Scalability Challenges in Web Search Engines* (Morgan & Claypool Publishers, 2015) 23. A web spider thinks that a page which contains a 404 error massages is not worth being indexed.

21 Aaron Schwabach, *Internet and the Law: Technology, Society, and Compromises, 2nd Edition: Technology, Society, and Compromises* (ABC-CLIO, 2014) 59. A form of indirect cybersquatting known as typosquatting which attempts to cash in on the traffic generated by high volume website.

22 Yi Pan, *Security in Distributed and Networking Systems* (World Scientific, 2007) 22. A domain is hijacked under the control of an attacker and the users are redirected to another website or webpage that an attacker targets also, DNS hijacking is also known as redirection.

23 Mark T. Carroll and American Law Institute-American Bar Association Committee on Continuing Professional Education, *ALI-ABA's Practice Checklist Manual on Advising Business Clients III: Checklists, Forms, and*

there is no direct legislation, which regulates cybersquatting in Australia. Instead, the conduct of falsely suggesting a connection between a registrant and their business is potentially caught by section 18 of the *ACL* in Queensland. Section 18 states that a person must not, in trade or commerce, engage in conduct that is misleading or deceptive or is likely to mislead or deceive.

The issue of "in trade and commerce" is well described in *Concrete Constructions (NSW) Pty Ltd v Nelson* ('*Concrete Case*').[24] The respondent ('worker') was employed by the appellant corporation ('the company'). He was injured after falling down an air conditioning shaft while attempting to remove a grate. He was told by the foreman that the grate was secured by three bolts so that it was safe to remove. He brought proceedings against the company for the breach of section 52 of the *Trade Practices Act 1974* (Cth) ('*TPA*'). The court ruled that foreman's conduct was not conduct in trade or commerce under section 52 of the *TPA* and allowed appeal. The majority chose narrower interpretation of 'in trade and commerce'. Under the narrow interpretation, 'in trade and commerce' is a conduct which is itself an aspect or element of activities or transactions which, of their nature, bear a trading or commercial character.[25] Unlike *Concrete Case*, SEO companies which provide BHSEO service to Australian consumers will be captured under section 18. Also, the term, 'trade or commerce', is defined in section 2(2) in the *ACL*, and states that the conduct of the business must be in trade or commerce within Australia or trade or commerce between Australia and a place outside. This is quite broad and thus will catch all SEO's working in Australia or with an Australian consumer.

To be caught under section 18, the conduct must also be misleading or deceptive or likely to mislead or deceive. In *Parkdale Custom Built Furniture P/L v Puxu P/L*,[26] the court

---

Advice from The Practical Lawyer (ALI-ABA, 2004) 359.

24 *Concrete Constructions (NSW) Pty Ltd v Nelson* (1990) 169 CLR 594.

25 *Concrete Constructions (NSW) Pty Ltd v Nelson* (1990) 169 CLR 594, [7].

26 *Parkdale Custom Built Furniture P/L v Puxu P/L* (1982) 149 CLR 191.

adopted an objective approach to determine whether the public at large was likely to be misled. Chief Justice Gibbs stated that the relevant person who may be misled is the reasonable member of the class directly affected by misleading or deceptive conduct. Here, if an article was properly labelled and displayed the name of the manufacturer, ordinary reasonable member of the public would not be misled: *Collins Marrickville Pty Ltd v Henjo Investments Pty Ltd & Ors.*[27]

The case of *CSR v Resource Capital Australia*[28] is an Australian 'cybersquatting' case where Colonial Sugar Refining Company ('CSR') produced raw sugar and exported it worldwide. They purchased the domain name, "www.csr.com.au/sugar", which contained information regarding their sugar, its production and recipes. In 2001, Resource Capital Australia Pty Limited ('RCA') registered both the domain name "csrsugar.com" and "constructionmaterials.com.au". They also registered the business domain name "Combined Sugar Retailers Sugar Supply ('CSR Sugar Supply') ". Then, RCA wrote a letter to CSR to offer to sell their domain name for approximately $30,000 but CSR did not accept the offer. Eventually, in September 2002, CSR's solicitors wrote a letter to RCA saying RCA was breaching the *TPA* and was passing off itself as having an association with CSR.[29] Justice Hill stated that RCA's actions were constituted as an example of cybersquatting since RCA's conduct in obtaining registration of the domain names constituted as misleading or deceptive conduct under section 52 of the *TPA*. RCA was subsequently ordered to restrain from using the domain names.

This case shows that if SEO companies purchase a batch of domain names that include competitor's domain names or other business names in order to get backlinks, it may be

---

27 *Collins Marrickville Pty Ltd v Henjo Investments Pty Ltd & Ors* (1987) ATPR 40.

28 *CSR Limited v Resource Capital Australia Pty Limited* [2003] FCA 279.

29 *CSR Limited v Resource Capital Australia Pty Limited* [2003] FCA 279, [38].

constituted as misleading or deceptive conduct. In this circumstance, the reasonable member of the class affected by misleading or deceptive conduct by using BHSEO are consumers and small business owners. The elements of misleading or deceptive conducts are successfully established.

3.2. Abusing Meta Tags

Google published the *Search Engine Optimisation Starter Guide*, which recommended the use of meta tags since Google might use them as snippets for website pages.[30] The meta tags[31] include meta titles, meta descriptions and meta keywords which are positioned in between the opening <head> and before the closing </head> in the HTML code.[32] In general, keywords, trademarks and popular products or services of the business are included in the meta title, meta description and meta keywords.[33] Jani McCutcheon said that there

30 Andrew Robertson and Michael Tilbury, *Divergences in Private Law* (Bloomsbury Publishing, 2016) 103. A snippets is a text excerpt, an image or a screenshot of a website which contains and displays information about pages or websites. Rich snippets tend to contain targeted keyword phrases without keywords stuffing.

31 Authors, Leanne Wiseman, et al stated in the *Australian Intellectual Property Law* that although internal users cannot see the meta tags, users rely on them to identify websites. In the past, meta tags only existed for search engines to perform search queries and for webmasters to increase their Google position but they are now also used as indicators for users to quickly identify websites at first glance.

32 The recommended of length of the meta-title is 69 characters which includes the spaces and the ideal length of the meta description is 160 characters.

33 Holly Mann, *Honest Riches* (Lulu.com, 2008) 93-98. Content Management Systems (CMS) allow users to add, update and edit contents of site without needing HTML coding. There are many types of CMS such as WordPress, Drupal, Joomla, Moodle, Geeklog, Zen Cart, PhpBB and etc. Nowadays, people create websites with Content Management System ('CMS') platforms. Among CMS platforms, WordPress is the most popular for web beginners to start with as it provides easy to install SEO plugins such as Yoast SEO and All in One. By using these plugins people are not required to know HTML codes since they automatically put the codes into the right position.

are inherent opportunities to abuse meta tags.[34] For instance, some businesses put the keywords of competitors in their meta tags to attract more visitors. They also put irrelevant keywords about products or services that they do not provide to increase website traffic or sales of products.[35] These behaviours are considered to be misleading or deceptive conduct.[36]

In Lift Shop Pty Ltd v Easy Living Home Elevators Pty Ltd ('*Lift Shop Case*'),[37] Lift Shop Pty Ltd (**'Lift Shop'**) and Easy Living Home Elevators (**'Easy Living'**) were direct competitors in the elevator industry. Easy Living hired a SEO marketing firm to modify it's website and improve it's Google ranking using SEO. The SEO firm asked Easy Living to choose five keywords and Easy Living chose the keyword 'lift shop'. Lift Shop argued that Easy Living appeared in the same SERP as them and alleged that using the keyword. 'Lift Shop', amounted to misleading or deceptive conduct under section 18 of the *ACL* and was also a trademark infringement. The court dismissed the application and stated that the keyword 'Lift shop' was used as a description, not a trademark. Justice Buchanan rejected the plaintiff's allegations that the defendant took part misleading and deceptive conduct as consumers could distinguish the plaintiff's business from the different URLs of the defendant's website. Also websites contained different title and description. To be captured under section 18 of the ACL, the plaintiff must prove that the other party engage in conduct that is mis-

34 Jani McCutcheon, 'Search and ye shall infringe? Current issues concerning the use and abuse of trade marks in cyberspace', (2006) 17 *AIPJ* 99.

35 *Complete Technology Integrations Pty Ltd v Green Energy Management Solutions* [2011] FCA 1319; *ACCC v Trading Post Australia Pty Ltd & Google Inc* [2011] FCA 1086. In *ACCC v Trading Post Australia Pty Ltd & Google Inc*, Trading Post used the competitor's keywords the head (meta title) of Google AdWords, and was sued for the breach of the misleading and deceptive conducts.

36 *Lift Shop Pty Ltd v Easy Living Home Elevators Pty Ltd* [2014] FCAFC 75. Lift Shop sued the Easy Living for the misleading and deceptive conduct under s 18 of the *Australian Consumer Law* and trade mark infringement.

37 *Lift Shop Pty Ltd v Easy Living Home Elevators Pty Ltd* [2014] FCAFC 75.

leading or deceptive or is likely to mislead or deceive. In this case, the plaintiff failed to prove there was anything to suggest any association between the two businesses.

The *Lift Shop case* is of significantly importance as it proves that Australian consumers and small business owners cannot be protected under the current *ACL* prohibition on misleading or deceptive conduct, even though they are directly impacted by falsely written meta tags of unregistered trademarks. They could end up losing their potential customers and profits. This case also clearly indicates that the importance of meta tags is under evaluated by judges.

3.3 Creating Fake Reviews to Receive Backlinks

Creating fake reviews is often a part of BHSEO strategy to receive backlinks.[38] Nowadays, it is easy to outsource SEO jobs to India, Bangladesh, Philippines or China. Many SEO experts from the micro job markets in third world countries will write fake reviews for a small fee ranging from one to ten dollars. They may also provide reviews even though they have not used the products or services.[39] They get backlinks from high PR sites so that they attract more traffic to websites, which is an important factor in terms of SEO strategy. Such actions including paid tweeting, are also arguably example of misleading or deceptive conduct under section 18 of the *ACL*.

Examples of where such behaviour has been deemed misleading or deceptive conduct include the conduct of the South Australian Tourist Commission when they paid

---

38 Matt McGee, *SEO Companies Fined Over Fake Reviews* (23 September 2013) <http://searchengineland.com/seo-companies-fined-over-fake-reviews-172526 >. One of the most common ways to get quality backlinks from the niche markets (narrow group) to pay online community owners, bloggers or webmasters to write promotional articles about products, or positive reviews of products or services.

39 The common platforms that they leave reviews on are Amazon, Apple App Store and Google Play Store.

celebrities to tweet their followers as if they had visited Kangaroo Island and had a good time even though they had not been to Kangaroo Island as claimed. The Australian Competition and Consumer Commission ('ACCC') said that celebrities do not have a duty to disclose paid sponsorships but such endorsements should not mislead people or make people think that celebrities have been somewhere if they have not.[40] Also, the ACCC took legal action against CityMove, which was penalised for a total of $30,600 because they had fabricated customer testimonials on Google Plus and YouTube.[41] These examples clearly shows that SEO companies which provide fake reviews for their clients (small business owners) are in breach of section 18 of the *ACL* if the fake review mislead consumers and cause loss or damages as a result of the deceptive conduct.

In *Australian Competition and Consumer Commission v P & N Pty Ltd*,[42] the Federal Court concluded that P & N Pty Ltd and P & N NSW Pty Ltd, which were trading under the name of "Euro Solar" and Worldwide Energy and Manufacturing Pty Ltd ('WEMA') which was known as "Australian Solar Panel", were liable for a penalty of $125,000 for their misleading and deceptive conduct. The court found that the company published fake testimonials as well as fake reviews on YouTube, testimonials and review which were not written by genuine customers of the companies. Also, the court added that the representation by P & N Pty Ltd and P & N NSW Pty Ltd was misleading or deceptive, or likely to mislead or deceive as the solar panels were made in Australia in fact they were made in China. In addition to this, Mr Nikunjkumar

40 Mark Pearson and Mark Polden, *The Journalist's Guide to Media Law: A handbook for communicators in a digital world* (Allen & Unwin, 2014), 462.

41 Frank Chung, *ACCC cracks down on fakes reviews* (30 July 2015) <http://www.news.com.au/finance/small-business/accc-cracks-down-on-fake-reviews/news-story/eb8d6c1fc7a2599a4ed4ec26ffe9fb2a>. This was in addition to a previous penalty of $6,600 they received in 2011, for publishing false testimonials on the website movingreview.com.au which is created by CityMove.

42 *Australian Competition and Consumer Commission v P & N Pty Ltd* [2014] FCA 6.

Patel, who was the sole director of P&N and WEMA received a court order to pay a fine of $20,000 because of his misleading conduct. The chairman of the ACCC, Rod Sims, said that this is a particularly important case which will set a yardstick in relation to fake reviews case, as it is the first successful litigation brought by the ACCC in this area.[43]

3.4 Sending or Attracting Fake Website Traffic

As shown, increasing website traffic is an important element for both WHSEO and BHSEO and can be a predictor of Google positioning. This means that a popular website which has a high volume of traffic may be placed in a good position on Google's SERP.[44] There are different types of web traffic such as organic traffic,[45] referral traffic,[46] direct traffic and paid traffic.[47] There are three common ways to attract website traffic. First, redirecting visitors using an URL shortener[48] that leads to a target website or webpage. Second, directly sending users or bot traffics to a target website or web

---

43 Australian Competition and Consumer Commission, *$145,000 penalty for fake testimonials and false solar energy country of origin representations* (17 January 2014) <https://www.accc.gov.au/media-release/145000-penalty-for-fake-testimonials-and-false-solar-energy-country-of-origin-representations>.

44 Alexa (www.alexa.com) provides traffic metrics and calculates the traffic ranking based on such parameters as reach and page views.

45 Organic traffic is the most ideal form of online marketing that most business owners prefer to use but it can be expensive and time-consuming to improve rankings on search engine sites this way.

46 Referral traffic is traffic where other websites refer or send the website traffic (online users) to targeted websites.

47 Susan Gunelius, *Content Marketing For Dummies* (John Wiley & Sons, 2011) 125. Paid traffic is traffic that business owners have paid to obtain. Paid traffic can be acquired through promoting online businesses, starting promotional campaigns sites such as on Pay Per Click ('PPC'), Google AdWords or paying money to high PR websites to get backlinks.

48 Many social media companies provide free URL shortener services. For example, Google provides goo.gl. It uses a 301 redirect which allows them to track their web traffic.

page.[49] Third, creating online banners and inducing people to click the banner to reach the targeted website. However, BHSEO professionals have began to abuse the shortener service, using it as a BHSEO tool that sends fake website traffic to a target website to increase website ranking.[50] They use the software to help them hijack users IP addresses or to send artificial bot traffic to a target website to increase the impression[51] as well as the search engine ranking by proxy.[52] In addition, they create online banners which are falsely designed and induce people to click the banner to send them to the targeted website. This is not real traffic and does not generate any sales.

Sending fake website traffic is one of BHSEO tactics which may be constituted as misleading or deceptive conduct under the *ACL*. Section 18 of the *ACL* states that a person must not, in trade or commerce, engage in conduct that is misleading or deceptive or is likely to mislead or deceive. In relation to the abuse of website traffic, the first question that arises is: Who can send the traffic? This is the most difficult threshold to meet in regards to section 18 of the *ACL* since it requires a high level of computing skills to find a wrongdoer who sends the fake web traffic. Once this element is proven then the complainant must also prove whether the wrongdoer is engaged in trade or commerce and prove that the conduct is misleading or deceptive because it misled people. Since, it is strenuous to find a person who send fake website traffic thus it is difficult to achieve under section 18. Currently, no cases involving sending fake website traffic are reported in Queensland.

49 Google may detect and doubt unmoral website traffic and gives penalty to a website. As a result, the website will not be indexed and will disappear from Google.

50 To avoid negative footages of a website, a lot of SEO experts prefer to use a URL shortener for their SEO campaign.

51 The definition of impression is how often ad is shown on a SERP on Google Network.

52 Igal Zeifman, *Report: Bot traffic is up to 61.5% of all website traffic* (9 December 2016) <https://www.incapsula.com/blog/bot-traffic-report-2013.html>.

In *Christophers Steelman v DoubleClick Inc and Delaware Business Corporation*,[53] people residing in the United States encountered a false advertising banner created by DoubleClick. DoubleClick is a lead marketing company in the U.S., creating more than 630 million ads for online business owners in 2002. The defendant created a Fake User Interface ("FUI") banner that fraudulently messaged users that there were computer system errors on their computers and hijacked their browser, taking them to the commercial website of DoubleClick. The plaintiff argued that the defendants had an intention to induce online users by making false, deceptive, or misleading representations of fact in the form of advertising banners disguised as computer alerts or system warnings. The Court award punitive damages against defendants in the amount of $500 per Class member in order to punish defendants for their misleading or deceptive conduct.

3.5 Spammy Link Building

Link building is a key SEO strategy. It is the act of spreading hyper-links which contain keywords or website URLs through as many niche markets[54] as possible and pointing the URLs back to the original site. Abuse of this link building strategy is called "link farming"[55] and is created through aggressive reciprocal linking.[56] Link building has the capacity to greatly impact a SERP ranking. It used to be an effective strategy for improving search engine ranking

53 *Christophers Steelman v DoubleClick INC and Delaware Business Corporation* (G.D. No. 03-12899) <http://www.ferencelaw.com/doubleclick/documents/certification.pdf>.

54 In the Cambridge dictionary, the word "niche market" is defined as a small area of trade within the economy, often involving specialized products.

55 Link farming techniques breach the Google Optimisation Guidelines and have a negative impact on the online market. They can also lead to de-indexing, which may result in the owner of a website receiving a penalty from Google.

56 Eric Enge, Stephan Spencer and Jessie Stricchiola, *The Art of SEO: Mastering Search Engine Optimization* ("O'Reilly Media, Inc.", 2015) 316.

in the past but it is no longer working since Google changed its algorithm and gives more awards for the quality of links rather than the quantity.[57]

In *Seikaly & Stewart v Rainmaker Institute*,[58] Seikaly & Stewart, a law firm in Michigan, brought a proceeding against Rainmaker Institute which is a SEO company specialising in online marketing using "spammy" techniques that did not comply with the Google Optimisation Guidelines. The plaintiff argued that the defendant knowingly performed the "spammy link farms" techniques in order to increase the website ranking of the plaintiff's law firm website.[59] They sought to recover $49,000 for their SEO service and also damages. Even though the plaintiff failed, this case is particularly important for not only small business owners but also legal practitioners in Australia. This is because there were no law suits regarding spammy link building techniques in Australia until *Oneflafre Pty Ltd v Chenih* [2016]. It opened the gate for small business owners and warned against the use of BHSEO.

Australia's most recent SEO case is *Oneflare Pty Ltd v Chernih*.[60] In this case, the plaintiff, Oneflare, ran an internet business which provided a matching service between services providers and potential customers. The plaintiff solely depended on search engines, primarily Google to obtain business. The plaintiff hired the first defendant, Mr. Chernih, a SEO expert, to run SEO to improve the plaintiff's website's "page ranking" so that their website would appears on the first page of Google. Later, the plaintiff also sued the defendant's company, Linkbuild. The plaintiff argued that

57 However, many people still believe that the quantity of links is an important part of SEO therefore, they still use software to leave 'spam links'.

58 *Seikaly & Stewart, P.C. v. Fairley*, 2014 WL 1911881 (D. Ariz. May 13, 2014).

59 Approximately, 6720 backlinks appeared and created for oaklandbusinesslawyers.com. However, all the links with the exception of approximately 188 links, were worthless links built with link farming techniques, and many backlinks were not forwarding to the plaintiff's web pages at all.

60 *Oneflare Pty Ltd v Chernih* [2016] NSWSC 1271.

the SEO techniques implemented by Mr. Chernih were contrary to Google's guidelines, and as a result the website was penalised and damages incurred. Despite the loss, Oneflare's claim against the defendants failed as the plaintiff's counsel could not persuade the judge that it caused significant damages to the plaintiff's business.

This will be a landmark case with regards to SEO in Australia as it addresses all BHSEO tactics as being conduct that may breach the *ACL*.[61] The case also demonstrates the emerging significant issues and confusion that the use of BHSEO is creating. A great number of SEO experts and IT professionals have debated whether "BHSEO is legitimate or not".[62] This is because BHSEO is a negative SEO strategy operated by software that does not comply with the Google Search Engine Optimisation Guideline. Companies using BHSEO, may also be in breach of the *ACL* and *IPL*.[63] If such laws fail to protect small business owners, they may be left with no recourse against a SEO company that they hire who, due to the use of BHSEO strategies, produce poor and unacceptable results.

To sum up, SEO companies which provide BHSEO strategies such as redirecting web customers to other websites, inserting competitor's keywords to appear in same SERP, creating fake reviews to receive backlinks and implementing spammy link building techniques will be engaged in misleading or deceptive conduct as they are in trade or commerce under the ACL.

---

61 The *ACL* is now in the Schedule 2 of the *Competition and Consumer Act 2010* (Cth) ('CCA'). Previously, it was captured under section 52, misleading and deceptive conduct of the *Trade Practices Act 1974* ('*TPA*').

62 whirlpool, *Black Hat SEO* (10 September 2013) <http://forums.whirlpool.net.au/archive/2119298>.

63 *Competition and Consumer Law Act 2010 (Schedule2 The Australian Consumer Law)*; *Trade Mark Act 1995* (Cth).

4. BREACH OF THE INTELLECTUAL PROPERTY LAW

THIS SECTION WILL DISCUSS ABOUT whether content farms techniques, using duplicated content violates the law under the *IPL*. Content farms are often used by companies who publish thousands of pieces of thin "news" to attract web users in search engines.[64] Similarly to the content farms, content scraping is often used as a SEO tool. When a person makes a copy of the original article without linking to the original source, this is considered as spam.

4.1 Content Farms and Duplicated Content

Panda was a new algorithm released on the 23rd of February 2011 by Google, which differed from previous algorithms in that it was constructed on site based instead of page based.[65] It affected all 12% of search results, cracking down on "thin websites" containing low quality contents, content farms as well as the site with high ad-to-content ratios.[66] In spite of such severe penalties given by Google,

64 Joseph Turow, Media Today: *Mass Communication in a Converging World* (Routledge, 2013) 8. Content farms are also known as "content mills" and are a BHSEO technique.

65 Vanessa Fox, *Marketing in the Age of Google, Revised and Updated: Your Online Strategy IS Your Business Strategy* (John Wiley & Sons, 2012) 152.

66 Darren Varndell, *Seo 2014: Includes How to Recover From Penguin, Panda or Manual Penalties* (2013) 74-86. Google penalty does not mean that a person violates the law. In particular, Google has penalised websites that use duplicate content and then pushed the affected website's

many people from micro job marketplaces spin articles with an article-spinning tool without the permission of the original owner then publishing them online or selling them to other small business owners.

In Australia, section 35(2) of the *Copyrights Act 1968* (Cth) defines the author of a work as the first owner of the copyright. When people use another's works that already exists it is called plagiarism, and is a breach of the original owner's copyright. To avoid such a breach, a person must reveal the original source of the material used. Under section 33 of the *Copyright Act*, a copyright in a published literary, dramatic, musical or artistic work expires 70 years after the death of the last author. Also, reproducing a substantial part of original work without the consent of the original owner(s) will be a breach of their copyright.[67]

While there are no specific cases that relate to the use of duplicate content from a website in Australia, there are some reported cases in the USA. In *D'Agostino v. Appliances Buy Phone, Inc.*,[68] D'Agostino, the plaintiff, and Appliances Buy Phones ('ABP'), the defendant, agreed that the plaintiff would build the defendant's e-commerce website.[69] Later, both parties entered in to a contract that the plaintiff would construct a second website with a different domain name ('Appliance4Sale') using the CMS platform.[70] Also, the both parties entered into an agreement under the name of the defendant with Google Merchant Center Terms of Service and agreed to comply with the Google Merchant

ranking down for any "thin" or "low quality" content.

67 Tina Hart, Simon Clark and Linda Fazzani, *Intellectual Property Law: Palgrave Law Masters* (Palgrave Macmillan, 2013) 166-168. The term "substantial" has been mentioned by Justice Finklestein in the *TCN Channel Nine Pty Ltd v Network Ten Pty Ltd* (2002) 118 FCR 417 where it was said *'there is no fixed rule for determining how much of a copyright work must be taken for it to be a substantial part of the work'*.

68 *D'Agostino v. Appliances Buy Phone Inc*, No. 15-1171 (3d Cir. 2015).

69 But they did not enter into an agreement for this project.

70 The second website was SEO optimised and the plaintiff received 50 percent of the commission generated from the second website.

Agreement to sell their products. From October 2009, both websites *www.ApplianceBuyPhone.com* ('first website') and *www.Appliance4Sale.com* ('second website') were operating separately at the same time so that the consumers could purchase the products from either of these websites. Until June 2010, the sales dramatically increased from the second website and as a result, ABP received over $30,000 worth of orders from the second website. Then, due to short supply, the defendant instructed the plaintiff to stop selling air conditioners, while the defendant continued to sell the products from the first website. This meant a reduction in the opportunities for the plaintiff to receive commission. Shortly after the defendant asked the plaintiff to stop selling, the second website was temporarily shut down due to the use of duplicate content, which breached the Google Merchant Agreement. Google penalised the second website for using duplicate content and halted website traffic to the second site. Around the same time, the defendant experienced glitches on the first website, and the defendant believed that the problem was related to Google's disapproval of the second website being duplicative. The defendants refused to pay the plaintiff for the development of the second website. This case proves that using duplicated content can cause damage not only to itself but also to the original website.[71] Since Google believes that they manipulate the search research, using duplicated content is constituted to be deceptive conducts.[72]

In *Donoghue v Allied Newspaper Ltd*,[73] Mr. Felstead interviewed Mr. Stephen Donoghue, who was a famous jockey in the United Kingdom. After interviewing him, Mr. Felstead published a series of articles with the title "Steve Donoghue's Racing Secrets, Enthralling Stories of the Sport of Kings" which was approved by Mr. Stephen Donoghue. Later, Mr.

71 Google deals seriously with duplicated content and announced that websites using duplicated content will be removed.

72 Google, *Duplicated content* <https://support.google.com/webmasters/answer/66359?hl=en>.

73 *Donoghue v Allied Newspaper Ltd* [1938] Ch 106.

Felstead published a new article using the previously published articles, but only changed the title to "My Racing Secrets" without Mr. Donoghue's consent. Mr. Donoghue brought forth proceedings to restrain any further forms of publication. The court ruled that Mr. Donoghue did not have a right to prevent the publication by Mr. Felstead. Despite Mr. Donoghue substantially influencing the works, the language used was by Mr. Felstead's, making him the author of the works.

Above cases shows that reproducing and reselling existing articles for the purpose of online publication is a breach of copyright law. Nowadays, technology has dramatically developed, and the plagiarism software can easily catch plagiarised sentences. A business owner should be aware of plagiarism and copyright issues when they write an article by themselves or when they hire SEO article writers.

5. LAW REFORM

WHILE IT HAS BEEN SHOWN that some avenues within the law exit for the regulation of BHSEO in Australia, reforms are required in order to prevent small business owners and consumers suffering damage from BHSEO provided by SEO companies.

5.1 Fake Reviews and Sending Fake Website Traffic

Currently, the misleading or deceptive conduct of creating fake reviews are well addressed by the ACCC. The ACCC developed a guide for business review platforms in 2013, which operates well in the modern society.[74] However, proving that the sending of fake website traffic is misleading or deceptive conduct under the *ACL* is difficult as the plaintiff must prove the detriment by another person's (those who send fake web traffic) dishonest behaviour. A Provisions in the *ACL* should be enacted that specifically make e-misleading and deceptive conduct, such as sending fake website traffic, a breach of the legislation.

---

74 Australian Competition and Consumer Commission, *What you need to know about: Online Reviews- guide for business and review platforms* (November 2013) < https://www.accc.gov.au/system/files/Online%20reviews%E2%80%94a%20guide%20for%20business%20and%20review%20platforms.pdf>.

5.2 Unauthorised Use of Unregistered Trademarks

In addition, the importance of the unauthorised use of unregistered trademarks in meta tags should be related to both lawyers and law students. To do so, law schools in Australia should provide a website development course as a compulsory subject while studying law school or legal professionals acquire special training for IT in practice. It may be considerable that the law society in each state should provide training courses for legal professionals to catch up with up-to-date technology; in particular, dealing with SEO legal issue to protect Australian small businesses. In *Oneflare Pty Ltd v Chernih*, if the legal professional had properly trained and had a special knowledge of SEO, it is likely that the plaintiff would have won the case.

5.3 Spam Links

There is no direct law to restrain the use of "spammy link-farming techniques" in Australia. The Australian case, *Oneflare Pty Ltd v Chernih* which dealt with spammy link-farming techniques claimed damages under the *Civil Liability Act 2002* (NSW), *TPA* and the *Fair Trading Act 1987* (NSW). In order to protect consumers and small business owners from BHSEO, spammy link building techniques should be regulated under the *Spam Act*. The phrase 'spam links' is excluded in the current definition clause, although most spam links includes the promotional messages or comments. To restrain SEO professionals from using 'spammy link building' techniques, section 6[75] and 17[76] of

75 Section 6 of the *Spam Act* defines 'commercial electronic message' as all types of advertising and promotional messages unless they are excluded by regulation. Currently, the phrase 'spam links' itself is not expressly described in this definition clause.

76 The 'spammy link building' tactic likely breaches section 17 of the *Spam Act*. According to this section, a commercial electronic message must contain certain information identifying the sender of the message and how they can be contacted. However, most messages or

the *Spam Act* should include the phrase 'spam link' so that Australian small business owners may have a broaden option to challenge against SEO companies to recover their loss.

comments that include spam links do not include this information since BHSEO experts often use auto-commenting software to spread identical comments on numerous websites.

CONCLUSION

IN 2016, THERE ARE MORE than one million websites on the World Wide Web; this means that it is significantly important to be ranked in a high position on search engine sites, in particular Google. Therefore, SEO is the key factor of a successful online business. However, some SEO companies provide BHSEO services using tactics such as cybersquatting, abusing meta tags, creating fake reviews, sending bot website traffic, implementing content farms and using spammy link building techniques that cause serious detriment to their customers who are generally small business owners or online consumers. These illegitimate activities cause the de-indexing of websites from search engine sites which leads to no sales of products or services. Currently, the ACCC, is the only organisation protecting online consumers and business owners from the misleading or deceptive conduct caused by BHSEO, but still many BHSEO tactics are not covered in any legislation. Therefore, the Australian Consumer Law and Intellectual Property Law should specifically regulate the BHSEO used by SEO companies in order to better protect consumers and small business owners.

REFERENCE

Articles/Books/Reports

Bailyn, Evan and Bardley Bailyn, *Outsmarting Google: SEO Secrets to Winning New Business* (Que Publishing, 2011)

Bezhovski, Zlatko, 'The Historical Development of Search Engine Optimization', (2015) 5(12) *Information and Knowledge Management* 92

Carroll, Mark T. and American Law Institute-American Bar Association Committee on Continuing Professional Education, *ALI-ABA's Practice Checklist Manual on Advising Business Clients III: Checklists, Forms, and Advice from The Practical Lawyer* (ALI-ABA, 2004)

Cambazoglu, B. Barla and Ricardo Baeza-Yates, *Scalability Challenges in Web Search Engines* (Morgan & Claypool Publishers, 2015)

Enge, Eric, Stephan Spencer and Jessie Stricchiola, *The Art of SEO: Mastering Search Engine Optimization* ("O'Reilly Media, Inc.", 2015)

Fox, Vanessa, *Marketing in the Age of Google, Revised and Updated: Your Online Strategy IS Your Business Strategy* (John Wiley & Sons, 2012)

Gunelius, Susan, *Content Marketing For Dummies* (John Wiley & Sons, 2011)

Hart, Tina, Simon Clark and Linda Fazzani, *Intellectual Property Law: Palgrave Law Masters* (Palgrave Macmillan, 2013)

Jani McCutcheon, 'Search and ye shall infringe? Current issues concerning the use and abuse of trade marks in cyberspace', (2006) 17 *AIPJ* 99

Jerkovic, John, *SEO Warrior* ("O'Reilly Media, Inc.", 2009)

Kae, Verens, *CMS Design Using PHP and jQuery : Build and Improve Your In-house CMS by Enhancing PHP with JQuery (1)* (Packt Publishing, 2010)

Leanne Wiseman and et al, *Australian Intellectual Property Law* (Cambridge, 3rd Ed, 2016)

Mann, Holly, *Honest Riches* (Lulu.com, 2008)

Mitchell, Scott, *Designing Active Server Pages* ("O'Reilly Media, Inc.", 2000)

Moran, Mike and Bill Hunt, *Search Engine Marketing, Inc.: Driving Search Traffic to Your Company's Website* (IBM Press, 2014)

Mbikiwa, F. and M. Wdideman,' Implications of search engine spam on the visibility of South African e-commerce Web site' (2006) Vol 8(4) *South African Journal of Information Management*

Moschovitis Group Staff, *Internet: A Historical Encyclopedia* (ABC-CLIO, 2005)

Odom, Sean, *Seo for 2011: Search Engine Optimization Secrets* (MediaWorksPublising.com, 2010)

Pan, Yi, *Security in Distributed and Networking Systems* (World Scientific, 2007)

Pearson, Mark and Mark Polden, *The Journalist's Guide to Media Law: A handbook for communicators in a digital world* (Allen & Unwin, 2014)

Perkins, Todd, *Search Engine Optimization for Flash: Best practices for using Flash on the web* ("O'Reilly Media, Inc.", 2009)

Pont, Gino Dal and Tina Cockburn, *Equity and Trust In Principle* (Thomson Reuters, 3rd Ed 2014)

Robertson, Andrew and Michael Tilbury, *Divergences in Private Law* (Bloomsbury Publishing, 2016)

Rognerud, Jon , *Ultimate Guide to Search Engine Optimization: Drive Traffic, Boost Conversion Rates and Make Lots of Money* (Jon Rognerud SEO, 2008)

Schwabach, Aaron, *Internet and the Law: Technology, Society, and Compromises, 2nd Edition: Technology, Society, and Compromises* (ABC-CLIO, 2014)

Turow, Joseph, Media Today: *Mass Communication in a Converging World* (Routledge, 2013)

Varndell, Darren, *Seo 2014: Includes How to Recover From Penguin, Panda or Manual Penalties* (2013)

Weber, Jonathan, *Practical Google Analytics and Google Tag Manager for Developers* (Apress, 2015) 186-187.

CASES

ACCC v Trading Post Australia Pty Ltd & Google Inc [2011] FCA 1086

Australian Competition and Consumer Commission v P & N Pty Ltd [2014] FCA

Collins Marrickville Pty Ltd v Henjo Investments Pty Ltd & Ors (1987) ATPR 40

Concrete Constructions (NSW) Pty Ltd v Nelson [1990] HCA 17

Complete Technology Integrations Pty Ltd v Green Energy Management Solutions [2011] FCA 1319

CSR Limited v Resource Capital Australia Pty Limited [2003] FCA 279

Donoghue v Allied Newspaper Ltd [1938] Ch 106

Lift Shop Pty Ltd v Easy Living Home Elevators Pty Ltd [2014] FCAFC 75

Mantra Group Pty Ltd v Tailly Ptdy Ltd (No 2) (2010) 86 IPR 19

Oneflare Pty Ltd v Chernih [2016] NSWSC 1271

Parkdale Custom Built Furniture P/L v Puxu P/L (1982) 149 CLR 191

Seikaly & Stewart, P.C. v. Fairley, 2014 WL 1911881

TCN Channel Nine Pty Ltd v Network Ten Pty Ltd (2002) 118 FCR 417

LEGISLATION

Competition and Consumer Law Act 2010 (Schedule2 The Australian Consumer Law)

Copyrights Act 1968 (Cth)

Trade Mark Act 1995 (Cth)

Trade Practices Act 1974 (Cth)

Spam Act 2003 (Cth)

TREATIES

Other

Aisha, Gani, *Amazon sues 1,000 'fake reviewers'* (18 October 2015) <https://www.theguardian.com/technology/2015/oct/18/amazon-sues-1000-fake-reviewers>

Australian Competition and Consumer Commission, *What you need to know about: Online Reviews- guide for business and review platforms* (November 2013) <https://www.accc.gov.au/system/files/Online%20reviews%E2%80%94a%20guide%20for%20business%20and%20review%20platforms.pdf>

Australian Competition and Consumer Commission, *$145,000 penalty for fake testimonials and false solar energy country of origin representations* (17 January 2014) <https://www.accc.gov.au/media-release/145000-penalty-for-fake-testimonials-and-false-solar-energy-country-of-origin-representations>

Chung, Frank, *ACCC cracks down on fakes reviews* (30 July 2015) <http://www.news.com.au/finance/small-business/accc-cracks-down-on-fake-reviews/news-story/eb8d6c1fc7a2599a4ed4ec26ffe9fb2a>

Gani, Aisha, *Amazon sues 1,000 'fake reviewers'* (18 October 2015) <https://www.theguardian.com/technology/2015/oct/18/amazon-sues-1000-fake-reviewers>

Google, *Duplicated content* <https://support.google.com/webmasters/answer/66359>

Frank Chung, *ACCC cracks down on fakes reviews* (30 July 2015) <http://www.news.com.au/finance/small-business/accc-cracks-down-on-fake-reviews/news-story/eb8d6c1fc7a2599a4ed4ec26ffe9fb2a>

Horn, Brian Ainsley, *Why Selling SEO is Unethical in 2016* (8 January 2016) <http://www.huffingtonpost.com/brian-horn/why-selling-seo-is-unethi_b_8929662.html>

McGee, Matt , *SEO Companies Fined Over Fake Reviews* (23 September 2013) <http://searchengineland.com/seo-companies-fined-over-fake-reviews-172526 >

Netcraft, *September 2016 Web Server Survey* (9 September 2016) <https://news.netcraft.com/archives/category/web-server-survey/>

Robin, Burton, *The Truth About Duplicate Content Issues in SEO* (24 March 2016) <http://seositecheckup.com/articles/the-truth-about-duplicate-content-issues-in-seo>

The Sydney Morning Herald, *Samsung fined for hiring bloggers to write fake reviews, attack rival HTC* (25 October 2013) <http://www.smh.com.au/digital-life/digital-life-news/samsung-fined-for-hiring-bloggers-to-write-fake-reviews-attack-rival-htc-20131025-2w5nx.html>

Zeifman, Igal, *Report: Bot traffic is up to 61.5% of all website traffic* (9 December 2016) <https://www.incapsula.com/blog/bot-traffic-report-2013.html>

BIBLIOGRAPHY

Article/ Books/ Journals

Afshari, Mostafa, *Affiliate Marketing Success-Step By Step Guide to Make 1000% ROI Using Dirt Cheap or Free Traffic Sources and Top Converting Affiliate Products* (eBookIt.com, 2015)

Barry Schwartz, *Law Firm Sues Their SEO Company For Using Spammy Tactics* (27 May 27 2014) <https://www.seroundtable.com/seo-sued-spam-18612.html>

Barry Taylor, *Cybersquatting: Defending Your Brand Name Just Got Way More Complicated* (16 June 2015)

<http://legal123.com.au/cybersquatting/>

Battelle, John. *The Search: How Google and Its Rivals Rewrote the Rules of Business and Transformed Our Culture*. New York: Portfolio. (September 2005)

Ben Elgin and et al, *Marketers thought the Web would allow perfectly targeted ads. Hasn't worked out that way* <http://www.bloomberg.com/features/2015-click-fraud/>

Berkman Klein Center, *Framing, Linking, and Metatags: Variation Three -- Metatags* <http://cyber.law.harvard.edu/metaschool/fisher/linking/metatags.html>

Bezhovski, Zlatko, 'The Historical Development of Search Engine Optimization', (2015) 5(12) *Information and Knowledge Management* 92

Carroll, Mark T. and American Law Institute-American Bar Association Committee on Continuing Professional Education, *ALI-ABA's Practice Checklist Manual on Advising Business Clients III: Checklists, Forms, and Advice from The Practical Lawyer* (ALI-ABA, 2004)

Cambazoglu, B. Barla and Ricardo Baeza-Yates, *Scalability Challenges in Web Search Engines* (Morgan & Claypool Publishers, 2015)

Clay, Bruce, *Search Engine Optimization All-in-One For Dummies* (John Wiley & Sons, 3rd 2015)

Danny Sullivan, *Meta Tag Lawsuits* (20 April 2004)

<https://searchenginewatch.com/sew/how-to/2064919/meta-tag-lawsuits>

Dean, Jeff (Google Senior Fellow). "Building Software Systems At Google and Lessons Learned" [video]. Stanford University, November 10, 2010.

Domain Name News, *$3.5 MILLION AWARDED IN TYPOSQUATTING CASE* (5 March 2013) <http://www.domainregistration.com.au/news/2013/1302-typosquatting-suit.php>

Eric Goldman, *Bad SEO Advice May Support Negligence Claim–D'Agostino v. Appliances Buy Phone* (21 September 2011) <http://blog.ericgoldman.org/archives/2011/09/bad_seo_advice.htm>

Fox, Vanessa, *Marketing in the Age of Google, Revised and Updated: Your Online Strategy IS Your Business Strategy* (John Wiley & Sons, 2012)

Greg Sterling, *Lawyers Sue SEO Firm For Violating GoogleGuidelines* (26 May 26 2014) <http://searchengineland.com/lawyers-sue-seo-firm-violating-google-guidelines-192492>

Gunelius, Susan, *Content Marketing For Dummies* (John Wiley & Sons, 2011)

Holston, David, *Design for Online Engagement: SEO, Content and Design Optimization for Editors and Designers* (HOW Books, 2013)

Jani McCutcheon, 'Search and ye shall infringe? Current issues concerning the use and abuse of trade marks in cyberspace', (2006) 17 *AIPJ* 99

Jerkovic, John, *SEO Warrior* ("O'Reilly Media, Inc.", 2009)

Jones, Kristopher B., *Search Engine Optimization: Your Visual Blueprint for Effective Internet Marketing* (John Wiley & Sons, 3rd Ed 2013)

Kae, Verens, *CMS Design Using PHP and jQuery : Build and Improve Your In-house CMS by Enhancing PHP with JQuery (1)* (Packt Publishing, 2010)

Kent, Peter, *SEO For Dummies* (John Wiley & Sons, 2015)

Leanne Wiseman and et al, *Australian Intellectual Property Law* (Cambridge, 3rd Ed, 2016)

Marie, Kristen, *MaFIA: Killer Marketing for Indie Authors* (eBookIt.com, 2013)

Mann, Holly, *Honest Riches* (Lulu.com, 2008)

Mbikiwa, F. and M. Wdideman,' Implications of search engine spam on the visibility of South African e-commerce Web site' (2006) Vol 8(4) *South African Journal of Information Management*

McCormick, Jason , *SEO Made Simple For 2011* (MediaWorksPublising.com, 2010)

Meyer, David. "Microsoft down to fifth place in comScore's global search stats, thanks to Yandex." GigaOM. February 6, 2013.

Mitchell, Scott, *Designing Active Server Pages* ("O'Reilly Media, Inc.", 2000)

Moran, Mike and Bill Hunt, *Search Engine Marketing, Inc.: Driving Search Traffic to Your Company's Website* (IBM Press, 2014)

Moschovitis Group Staff, *Internet: A Historical Encyclopedia* (ABC-CLIO, 2005)

Odom, Sean, *Seo for 2011: Search Engine Optimization Secrets* (MediaWorksPublising.com, 2010)

Sostre, Pedro and Jennifer LeClaire, *Web Analytics For Dummies* (John Wiley & Sons, 2007)

Sullivan, Danny. "Google: 100 Billion Searches Per Month, Search To Integrate Gmail, Launching Enhanced Search App For iOS." Search Engine Land. August 8, 2012.

Sullivan, Danny. "Google Still World's Most Popular Search Engine By Far, But Share Of Unique Searchers Dips Slightly." Search Engine Land. February 11, 2013.

Waelde, Charlotte et al, *Contemporary Intellectual Property: Law and Policy* (Oxford University Press, 2016)

Vermaat, Misty E., *Discovering Computers, Essentials ©2016* (Cengage Learning, 2015)

CASE

ACCC v Trading Post Australia Pty Ltd & Google Inc [2011] FCA 1086

Australian Competition and Consumer Commission v P & N Pty Ltd [2014] FCA

Brambles Holdings Ltd v Bathurst City Council (2001) 53 NSWLR 153

Collins Marrickville Pty Ltd v Henjo Investments Pty Ltd & Ors (1987) ATPR 40

Concrete Constructions (NSW) Pty Ltd v Nelson [1990] HCA 17

Commercial Union Assurance Company of Australia Ltd v Ferrcom Pty Ltd (1991) 22 NSWLR 389

Complete Technology Integrations Pty Ltd v Green Energy Management Solutions [2011] FCA 1319

County Securities Pty Ltd v Challenger Group Holdings Pty Ltd [2008] NSWCA 193

CSR Limited v Resource Capital Australia Pty Limited [2003] FCA 279

Donoghue v Allied Newspaper Ltd [1938] Ch 106

Lift Shop Pty Ltd v Easy Living Home Elevators Pty Ltd [2014] FCAFC 75

Liverpool City Council v Irwin [1977] AC 239

Mantra Group Pty Ltd v Tailly Ptdy Ltd (No 2) (2010) 86 IPR 19

Oneflare Pty Ltd v Chernih [2016] NSWSC 1271

Parkdale Custom Built Furniture P/L v Puxu P/L (1982) 149 CLR 191

Prestia v Aknar (1996) 40 NSWLR 165

Seikaly & Stewart, P.C. v. Fairley, 2014 WL 1911881

TCN Channel Nine Pty Ltd v Network Ten Pty Ltd (2002) 118 FCR 417

Wallace v Kam (2013) 250 CLR 375

Watson v Foxman (1995) 49 NSWLR 315

LEGISLATION

Competition and Consumer Law Act 2010 (Schedule2 The Australian Consumer Law)

Copyrights Act 1968 (Cth)

Criminal Code 1899 (Qld)

Trade Mark Act 1995 (Cth)

Trade Practices Act 1974 (Cth)

Spam Act 2003 (Cth)

TREATIES

others

Morris, Aaron, *My Experience with Stephen Fairley and The Rainmaker Institute* (8 September 2016) <http://practiceoflawblog.com/my-experience-with-stephen-fairley-and-the-rainmaker-institute/>

Attorney General Eric T. Sch neiderman, *A.G. Schneiderman Announces Agreement With 19 Companies To Stop Writing Fake Online Reviews And Pay More Than $350,000 In Fines* (23 September 2013) <http://www.ag.ny.gov/press-release/ag-schneiderman-announces-agreement-19-companies-stop-writing-fake-online-reviews-and>

Aull, Jacob, *WordPress SEO Success: Search Engine Optimization for Your WordPress Website or Blog* (Que Publishing, 2014)

Schwartz, Barry, *Law Firm Sues Their SEO Company For Using Spammy Tactics* (27 May 27 2014) <https://www.seroundtable.com/seo-sued-spam-18612.html>

Taylor, Barry, *Cybersquatting: Defending Your Brand Name Just Got Way More Complicated* (16 June 2015) <http://legal123.com.au/cybersquatting/>

Elgin, Benand et al, *Marketers thought the Web would allow perfectly targeted ads. Hasn't worked out that way*
<http://www.bloomberg.com/features/2015-click-fraud/>

Berkman Klein Center, *Framing, Linking, and Metatags: Variation Three -- Metatags*
<http://cyber.law.harvard.edu/metaschool/fisher/linking/metatags.html>

Buesing, Dave , *What To Do About a Fake BS Surge of Google Analytics Visits* (16 February 2013)
<http://davebuesing.com/google-analytics-spam-traffic-bots/>

Sullivan, Danny, *Meta Tag Lawsuits* (20 April 2004)
<https://searchenginewatch.com/sew/how-to/2064919/meta-tag-lawsuits>

Domain Name News, $3.5 *MILLION AWARDED IN TYPOSQUATTING CASE* (5 March 2013)
<http://www.domainregistration.com.au/news/2013/1302-typosquatting-suit.php>

Goldman, Eric, *Bad SEO Advice May Support Negligence Claim–D'Agostino v. Appliances Buy Phone* (21 September 2011)
<http://blog.ericgoldman.org/archives/2011/09/bad_seo_advice.htm>

Sterling, Greg, *Lawyers Sue SEO Firm For Violating GoogleGuidelines* (26 May 26 2014)
<http://searchengineland.com/lawyers-sue-seo-firm-violating-google-guidelines-192492>

Haynes, Marie, *Negative SEO: Should You Be Worried? If Attacked, What Should You Do?* (26 August 2014) <https://moz.com/blog/preparing-for-negative-seo>

Hom Brian Anisley, *Why Selling SEO Is Unethical in 2016* (01 August 2016) <http://www.huffingtonpost.com/brian-horn/why-selling-seo-is-unethi_b_8929662.html>

Colville, Iain, *Can you sue your SEO agency?* (22 December 2015) <https://www.wrighthassall.co.uk/knowledge/legal-articles/2015/12/22/can-you-sue-your-seo-agency/>

Swede, James, *Disputes with SEO companies* (5 November 2013) <http://www.darlingtons.com/blog/disputes-with-seo-companies>

Edwards, Jim, *Google Sued Over Conspiracy Theory That It Defrauded Thousands Of Publishers Of Ad Money* (21 May 2014) <http://www.businessinsider.com.au/google-adsense-class-action-lawsuit-2014-5?r=US&IR=T>

Kotaw, Katherine, *Can you Sue Your SEO for Black Hat Tactics? It's a Gray Area* (6 August 201) <http://www.sitepronews.com/2013/08/06/can-you-sue-your-seo-for-black-hat-tactics-its-a-gray-area/>

Evans, Kimberley, *Online Copyright Infringement: Recent Cases Worldwide and Legislative response* (1 November 2010) <http://www.davies.com.au/ip-news/online-copyright-infringement-recent-cases-worldwide-and-legislative-respon>

O'reilly, Lara, *Ad tech company Criteo says its rival SteelHouse ran a 'counterfeit click fraud scheme'* (14 Jun 2016) <http://www.businessinsider.com.au/criteo-vs-steelhouse-click-fraud-lawsuit-2016-6>

Dunham, Marianne and Jason Watson, *Cybersquatting; typosquatting – Facebook's $2.8 million in damages and domain names* (10 May 2013) <http://www.lexology.com/library/detail.aspx?g=7088bf09-8a9e-4449-a179-d90bdfad3310>

Ingram, Mathew, *There's a ticking time bomb inside the online advertising market* (1 July 2015) <http://fortune.com/2015/07/01/online-advertising-fraud/>

McFadden Ticen & Beam, *How To Sue A SEO Company* (17 October 2014) <http://www.breachofcontractarizona.com/sue-seo-company/>

McGee, Matt, *SEO Companies Fined Over Fake Reviews* (23 September 2013) <http://searchengineland.com/seo-companies-fined-over-fake-reviews-172526>

Kuepper, Michelle, *COPYING WEBSITES – HOW FAR CAN YOU LEGALLY GO?* <http://theheureka.com/copying-websites>

Schwartz, Noam, *Are Bots Hijacking Your Marketing Budget?* (3 October 2014) <https://techcrunch.com/2014/10/03/are-bots-hijacking-your-marketing-budget/>

OUT-LAW.com, *Meta tag abusers face 20 years in prison* (28 July 2006) <http://www.theregister.co.uk/2006/07/28/us_meta_tag_law/>

Parsons, James, *Does Buying Traffic Hurt Your Google Rankings?* (24 August 2014) <http://growtraffic.com/blog/2014/08/buying-traffic-hurt-google-rankings>

Roesler, Peter, *Google Sues Unethical SEO Company for Unethical Business Practices* (22 September 2015) <http://www.webmarketingpros.com/blog/google-sues-unethical-seo-company-for-unethical-business-practices/>

Glover, Sam, *Law Firm Sues the Rainmaker Institute for Failed SEO [UPDATED]* (29 July 2013) <https://lawyerist.com/67836/law-firm-sues-the-rainmaker-institute-for-failed-seo/>

Scott, Samuel, *The Alleged $7.5 Billion Fraud in Online Advertising* (22 June 2015) <https://moz.com/blog/online-advertising-fraud>

Bird, Sarah, *The Jones Day Lawsuit: Mega Law Firm Sues E-Commerce Site For Linking Back To It* (13 October 2008) <https://moz.com/blog/the-jones-day-lawsuit-big-law-firm-sues-ecommerce-site-for-linking-back-to-it>

Bird, Sarah, *Washington State Sues SEO Company Visible.net* (14 November 2008) <https://moz.com/blog/washington-state-sues-seo-company-visiblenet>

Datoo, Siraj, *France drops controversial 'Hadopi law' after spending millions* (10 July 2013) <https://www.theguardian.com/technology/2013/jul/09/france-hadopi-law-anti-piracy>

Smoot, Scott, *Why Multiple Domains Are Mostly Bad For SEO* (5 January 2011) <https://www.seo.com/blog/multiple-domains-seo/>

Sunshine Coast Daily, *The dark art of blackhat SEO* (14 July 2010) <http://www.sunshinecoastdaily.com.au/news/dark-art-blackhat-seo-search-engine-google/583311/>

Swede, James, *Disputes with SEO companies* (5 November 2013) <http://www.darlingtons.com/blog/disputes-with-seo-companies>

Tahan, Mohammad, *Beginner's Guide to SEO: Simple training web site optimization for search engines* (2016,)

Tina Courtney, *4 Mighty SEO Tools Built for Small Businesses* (23 September 23 2016) <http://www.sitepronews.com/2016/09/23/4-mighty-seo-tools-built-for-small-businesses/>

The Search Ninjas, *Law Firm Sues SEO Provider* (31 July 2013) <http://www.thesearchninjas.com/law-firm-sues-seo-provider>

The Sydney Morning Herald, *Cyber-squatting cases reach record high* (29 March 2013) <http://www.smh.com.au/it-pro/business-it/cybersquatting-cases-reach-record-high-20130329-2gy5b.html>

Truro Solicitors, *Cornwall Litigation : SEO claims* (27 May 2014) <http://lawincornwall.co.uk/cornwall-litigation-seo-claims/>

Twomey, David P. et al, *Business Law: Principles for Today's Commercial Environment* (Cengage Learning, 2016)

Zebida, Hesham , *Why Fake Traffic Sucks and How it Hurts Your Business Blog* <http://famousbloggers.net/fake-traffic.html>

5030LAW LAW RESEARCH ELECTIVE 2016

Annex 2

Research Plan

Student Name: Park, Adrienne (KJ)

(Last name) (First name / initials)

Student Number:

Email Address:

Supervisor: Mr. Aidan Booker

Course

5030LAW (Research Elective)

1. *Legal Areas of Study & Research*

- Consumer Law
- Intellectual Property
- Contract Law

2. *Non-Legal Areas of Study & Research*

(optional for 5030LAW students)

- Information Technology
- Online Marketing

3. *Working Title*

Note: your title should clearly communicate the topic of your project, but can be changed or refined in your later work

- White, Grey or Black Search Engine Optimisation (SEO) under the Australian Consumer Law and Intellectual Property Law.

4. *Research Question(s)*

(This can continue to be changed or refined in your later work)

- How the Australian Consumer Law and Intellectual Property Law can be used to regulate the White Hat SEO, Grey Hat SEO and Black Hat SEO used by SEO companies to better protect consumers and small business owners?

5. *Significance*

Nowadays, more than 77 percent of internet users use Google to search for products or services. This means that approximately 1.17 billion users use Google every single day and over 3.5 billion searches are performed. These statistics suggest that over 40,000 search queries are performed every second on average and that Google performs 1.2 trillion search queries annually. Due to the economic recession, a large number of people established online businesses, as they do not require large amounts of capital to start, there is a low risk of failure and they are easy to operate and maintain. Nowadays, everyone can open online shops within a few seconds by using Content Management System ('CMS') platforms such as WordPress, Drupal, Wix, Joomla and other free CMS platforms. However, not everyone will succeed. Even though they open a fancy website, if the site is not properly indexed as a result of de-indexing, they will sell no services or products.

For this reason, Search Engine Optimisation ('SEO') companies have become a key part of ensuring the success of online businesses. Most online business owners are aware of this fact and are paying to attract more online users (web traffic) by hiring SEO experts. Because of SEO's characteristics, SEO services must be performed for at least 3 months. In general, it takes 12 months to see successful SEO results that will lead to substantial revenue increases.

There are 3 types of SEO strategies: White Hat SEO, Black Hat SEO, and Grey Hat SEO. White Hat SEO is a positive Search Engine Optimisation strategy operated by a human that improves the search engine performance on a Search Engine Result Page('SERP'). For instance, press releases, social media campaigns, article submission to the high Page Rank('PR') websites and Google AdWords Campaigns are included. In contrast, Black Hat SEO is a negative search engine optimisation strategy operated by software that do not comply with the Google Search Engine Optimisation Guideline as well as the Australian Consumer Law and the Intellectual Property Law. For instance, article submission after article spinning with a spinning tool, sending fake web traffic with software to increase the Google position and leaving spam comments on websites with auto commenting software.

In general, ethical companies will only use the White Hat SEO strategy but many SEO companies use a mixture of White Hat SEO and Black Hat SEO, which is called Grey

Hat SEO. Unfortunately, there are many SEO companies that fail to reach their intended achievement within a certain period of time for many reasons. For instance, they may use software which generates spam links, implement 'Black Hat SEO' by using the software or commit a breach of Intercultural Property Law as many SEO experts are not good at law.

Although small business owners can hire a SEO company and still have poor results, a great number of them cannot be refunded for their expenses as there are few relevant laws with respect to this issue. In the near future, an increasing amount of people will start online businesses and SEO is a necessary tool to implement prior to opening. In this respect, I believe that small business owners/consumers need protection from SEO companies charging for services and not producing positive results because they do not provide the service they promise. We need online small business owners to be successful to boost the Australian economy. In this research paper, I will review and analyse the current Australian Consumer law, Australian Intellectual Property Law and Contract law. I will also suggest possible legal actions that small business owners can possibly take against such SEO companies, under the laws mentioned above, so that they can protect themselves from financial risk and damages.

6. *Methodology*

The following steps will be taken:

Step 1: Formulating research problem

- What is Search Engine Optimisation?
    - » The definition of White Hat SEO, Black Hat SEO and Grey Hat SEO

Step 2: Extensive literature research as to Search Engine Optimisation ('SEO')

- Collect information, in particular " Black Hat SEO" strategies from:
  - » Text Books
  - » Legal documents
  - » Journals
  - » Cases
  - » Google Search Engine Optimisation Guideline

Step 3: Examining and review current relevant laws of the Australian Consumer Law ('ACL')

- Legal dictionary
- Legislations
- Cases
- ACCC website

Step 4: Examining and review current relevant laws of the Intellectual Property ('IP')

- Legal dictionary
- Legislations
- Cases
- World Intellectual Property Organization
- IP Australia

Step 5: Find and compare the relevant cases:

- in Europe
- in Australia
- in Queensland

Step 6: Suggest law reform and find the alternative solutions

7. Ethics

(Is ethical clearance needed for this research? Check using the procedures under 'Research Ethics' on the course site at Learning@Griffith. This question will usually only arise if you are conducting empirical research (e.g. surveying or interviewing people, especially people from vulnerable groups) or seeking to access or use confidential information, and may wish to use your final people for any purposes other than assessment (e.g. circulation or publication).

If clearance is required, an Ethics Application in the required form must be attached to this Research Plan.) (Mark/tick one)

- No clearance required
- Clearance required; application attached

(Copy the application into the end of this document. Supervisors will review and consult with the convenors who will give (or withhold) formal approval under the University's ethical clearance arrangements.)

8. Preliminary bibliography

Articles/Books/Reports

Darren Varndell, *SEO SOS: Search Engine Optimization First Aid Guide ePub eBook* (Lulu Press, Inc, 2014)

Davison Mark, Ann Monotti and Leanne Wiseman, *Australian Intellectual Property Law* (Cambridge University Press, 3rd ed, 2016)

Fitzgerald, Brian et al, *Internet and E-commerce Law* (Thomson Reuters, 2nd ed, 2011)

Harry Knightm, 'Veda Advantage case clarifies Australian trade mark law on Google AdWords' (2016) 19(5-6) INTLB 366

Longden, James Alexander, 'Trade mark use and misleading advertising in Google AdWords: A comparative analysis of search engine liability in Australia and Europe' (2014) 25(1) AIPJ 35

Mahmoud, Mando, 'Invisible trademark infringement and passing off on the internet: Meta-tags, search engines, initial interest confusion and reform' (2015) 26 AIPJ 75

Paul Kallenbach and Fahim Ahad, 'Sponsored links and trade mark litigation: possible approaches in Australia' (2005) 8(8) INTLB 109

Wynne, Paula, *Pimp My Site: The DIY Guide to SEO, Search Marketing, Social Media and Online PR* (John Wiley & Sons, 2012)

Legislation

Competition and Consumer Law Act 2010 (Schedule2 The Australian Consumer Law)

Copyright Act 1968 (Cth)

Privacy Act 1998 (Cth)

The Spam Act 2003 (Cth)

Trade Mark Act 1995 (Cth)

Trade Practices Act 1974 (Cth)

Cases

Accor Australia & New Zealand Hospitality Pty Ltd v Liv Pty Ltd (2015)112 IPR 494

Cosmetic Warriors Limited and Lush Limited v Amazon.co.uk Limited and Amazon EU SARL [2014] EWHC 181

Interflora Inc & Anor v Marks and Spencer Plc [2014] EWCA Civ 1403

Mantra Group Pty Ltd v Tailly Pty Ltd (No 2) [2010] FCA 291

Tasman Insulation New Zealand Limited v Knauf Insulation Limited & Ors [2014] NZHC 960

Treaties

Paris Convention for the Protection of Industrial Property, adopted on 20 March 1883, (entered into force 27 September, 1975)

Patent Law Treaty, adopted on 1 June 2000 , (entered into force April 28, 2005)

Trademark Law Treaty, adopted on October 27 1994 , (entered into force August 1, 1996)

WIPO Copyright Treaty, adopted on December 20 1996, (entered into force May 20, 2002)

Other

Brendan Gibbons, *Search Engines, Indexing and Copyright Law* (14 December 2009) <http://www.practicalecommerce.com/articles/1457-Search-Engines-Indexing-and-Copyright-Law>

Christine Ecob & Sarah McKeith, *Search engine optimisation and trade mark infringement under Australian law* (October 2014) <http://www.jws.com.au/en/acumen/item/520-search-engine-optimisation-and-trade-mark-infringement-under-australian-law>

Frank Chung, *ACCC cracks down on fake reviews* (30 July 2015) <http://www.news.com.au/finance/small-business/accc-cracks-down-on-fake-reviews/news-story/eb8d6c1fc7a2599a4ed4ec26ffe9fb2a>

Made in the USA
Monee, IL
04 November 2026

67382359R00046